THE RIPPL
A KINDNESS JOURNAL
TO SPARK JOY AND COMPASSION

Feeling kindness is different for everyone.
Acts of kindness can include actions, an items, or even feelings.

One thing everyone does agree on, is that
kindness can fill you with positive emotions.

We first learn about kindness as helping and sharing. As we grow, we start to understand that kindness is an important piece of relationship building. Whether we are building relationships with others, ourselves, or the world around us, kindness becomes an important piece of the relationship growth.

Through encouragement and practice, everyone can build a stronger kindness habit, making it a part of their daily lives.

Did you know that acts of kindness encourage more kindness?
A "pay it forward" action is a kind act by one person that
encourages someone else to show kindness, too.

This is the beginning of a Kindness Ripple Effect.

People who practice kindness every day are more likely to
be happier and more resilient.

SHARING KINDNESS WITH OTHERS WILL MAKE THE WORLD A BETTER PLACE!

THE RIPPLE EFFECT
A KINDNESS JOURNAL
TO SPARK JOY AND COMPASSION

More books, journals, & resources:
Visit: www.MightyMindsets.com

Please leave a review of this book on Amazon.
We would love to know your thoughts, opinions,
& comments to better improve our products.

Copyright © 2024 by Bethany C. Goding
ISBN: 978-1-958765-15-9

All rights reserved. No part of this book may be reproduced or used in any manner without written permission of the copyright owner except for the use of quotations in a book review. For more information, address: Bethany@mightymindsets.com

Mighty Mindsets, LLC
River Road
Tenants Harbor, Maine
United States of America

Copyright © 2024 Bethany C. Goding
WWW.MIGHTYMINDSETS.COM

THE RIPPLE EFFECT
A KINDNESS JOURNAL
TO SPARK JOY AND COMPASSION

USING THE JOURNAL

This journal is designed to help you strengthen your kindness muscles.

The activities are designed to build kindness habits and skills.
As you write, take the time to reflect on your thoughts.
Have fun as you learn about yourself and the people you love.

**The journal prompts and activities in this book provide
the stepping stones to positive kindness habits.**

Find People to Show Kindness To
When you first start to practice kindness, it is easier to show
kindness to people we know and care about.

Identify Acts of Kindness
This type of reflection allows you to think about the people around you and try to understand what they need. It's also important to look within yourself to find how the skills you possess can help others.

Kindness Reflections
When you're growing your kindness habit, it's important to think about the kindness you have shown. The true meaning of kindness tends to come out in a written reflection. These guided prompts will help the you see things from a different perspective, as you learn about yourself.

This Journal Contains
Over 60 Kindness Writing Prompts
Over 35 Kindness Quote Reflection Prompts
5 "Create Your Own" Acts of Kindness Lists
20 Acts of Kindness & Reflection Writing Prompts

> How wonderful is it that no one need wait a single minute before starting to improve the world.
> Anne Frank

Showing kindness to others will help you in many ways.

**Build relationships
Increase self esteem
Develop empathy
Physical benefits
Boosts happiness**

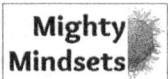

THE RIPPLE EFFECT

What does kindness mean to you?
When you hear the word *kindness*, what do you think of first?

_____
_____
_____
_____
_____
_____
_____
_____

What actions make you think of kindness?

_____
_____
_____
_____
_____

Create a list of people you would like to show kindness.
Don't forget to include yourself on this list!

1. _____

2. _____

3. _____

4. _____

5. _____

6. _____

7. _____

8. _____

Create a list of people who have shown you kindness.

1. _____

2. _____

3. _____

4. _____

5. _____

6. _____

7. _____

8. _____

When you think of kindness, what words come to mind?
Add to the word cloud below.

family

friendship

happiness

helping

What actions remind you of kindness?

Writing a thank you note

HOLD THE DOOR OPEN FOR SOMEONE

GIVE SOMEONE A COMPLIMENT

What are some acts of kindness you have shown?

What inspired you to show kindness?

Share a moment when someone showed you kindness.

_____
_____
_____
_____
_____
_____
_____
_____

How did receiving kindness make you feel?

Consider someone in your life you see as kind.
What specific qualities or actions does this person demonstrate that reflect their kindness?

_____
_____
_____
_____
_____
_____
_____
_____

What traits do you have in common?

Describe a time when you showed kindness.

How did showing kindness make you feel?

Recall a moment when you found it tough to be kind.
Write about how the other person might
have felt in that situation.

_____
_____
_____
_____
_____
_____
_____

**What can you do differently next time to show
understanding and kindness, even when it's not easy?**

_____
_____
_____
_____
_____
_____
_____

Think about a time when being kind was hard for you.
What happened, and how did it make you feel?
Was there a way you could have handled it differently?

_____

_____

_____

_____

Share your thoughts on how you can turn challenges into opportunities for kindness.

Imagine kindness as a puzzle, and sometimes the pieces are tricky to fit together.

Describe a time when being kind felt like solving a puzzle. How did you eventually piece it together?

_____
_____
_____
_____
_____
_____
_____

Reflect on the importance of patience and creativity in finding kind solutions to challenging situations.

_____
_____
_____
_____
_____
_____
_____

What is a kindness "Ripple Effect"?

Imagine you do something kind for a friend.
How do you think that makes them feel?
Now, think about how your kindness might spread to others around you, just like ripples in a pond.

_____

_____

_____

_____

_____

_____

Reflect on the idea that small acts of kindness can create a big impact and make the world a better place.

**Consider each kind act as a stone thrown into a pond.
Picture the ripples expanding and touching others.
What kind things have you done recently, and how do you think they might have affected people around you?**

_____
_____
_____
_____
_____
_____
_____

Reflect on the idea that kindness has a way of spreading, creating positive waves in the world.

_____
_____
_____
_____
_____
_____
_____
_____

Consider a time when someone's kindness affected you.
How did it make you feel?
Now, imagine if everyone around you did small acts of kindness.
How might that create a huge wave of positivity?

Reflect on the power you have to contribute to this wave and make the world a kinder place.

**Think about a famous person you admire.
Can you recall a time when they showed kindness
or made a positive impact on others?
Describe the situation and how their actions influenced you.**

_____

_____

_____

_____

_____

_____

_____

**Consider how acts of kindness from celebrities can
inspire people all around the world.**

Imagine your favorite celebrity as a kindness superhero.
Reflect on a specific act of kindness they've done or a cause they've supported.
How does their kindness make them a hero in your eyes?

_____

_____

_____

_____

_____

Consider how their actions might motivate you to spread kindness in your own way.

_____

_____

_____

_____

_____

_____

Picture kindness as magical seeds that, when planted, grow into beautiful flowers.
Reflect on how each kind action is like planting a seed of goodness.

_____

_____

_____

_____

_____

_____

_____

How can your acts of kindness contribute to a garden of positivity that blossoms not just around you but all over the world?

_____

_____

_____

_____

_____

Imagine you're on a secret mission to spread kindness.
Reflect on different ways you can secretly and anonymously do something nice for someone else. Consider the joy and surprise it might bring.

_____
_____
_____
_____
_____
_____

How can you turn your everyday actions into small acts of kindness that create a ripple effect?

Reflect on the impact your words can have.
Consider writing a kind and encouraging note to someone, whether it's a friend, family member, or even a teacher.

How can your words inspire others to show kindness, creating a positive environment for everyone?

_____

_____

_____

_____

_____

Consider kindness as a reflection of who we are.
Reflect on how being kind to others is like looking in a mirror and seeing the goodness within ourselves.

How can acts of kindness teach us about our own values and the positive impact we can have on the world?

**Picture yourself as a kindness ninja,
silently spreading good vibes.**
**Reflect on an act of kindness you can perform
without revealing your identity.**

How can acts of kindness teach us about our own values and the positive impact we can have on the world?

_____
_____
_____
_____
_____
_____
_____

**Think about someone in your life who could use
a little extra kindness this week.
Reflect on a specific kind action you can plan for them.**

**How can you create a plan for kindness that will make
them smile or brighten their day?**

Imagine taking a walk in someone else's shoes.
Reflect on how accepting people for who they are involves understanding their feelings and experiences.

_____

_____

_____

_____

How can you practice empathy and openness to truly appreciate and accept others just as they are?

Think about ways you can be kind without anyone knowing it was you.
Reflect on how these invisible acts of kindness can bring happiness to others. What's a simple, anonymous act you can do to make someone's day a little brighter?

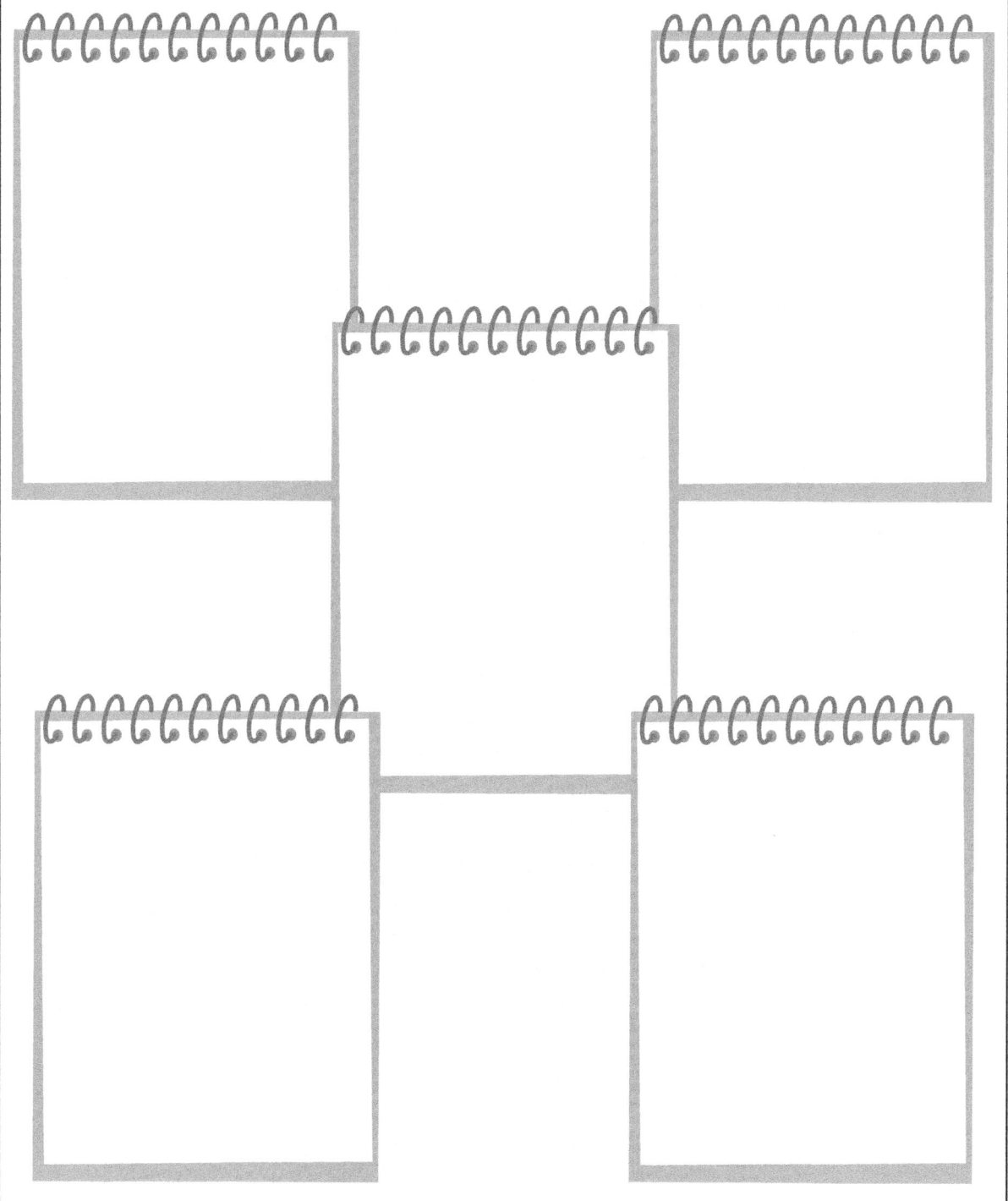

Think about the diverse colors of a rainbow, each unique and beautiful in its own way.

Reflect on how accepting people for who they are is like celebrating the different colors in your friendships.

How can you appreciate and value the unique qualities that each friend brings to your life?

Consider the power of a million-dollar smile.

Reflect on how you can bring joy to others through simple acts of kindness, whether it's sharing toys, helping someone in need, or spreading positivity.

How can your actions create a world filled with smiles and happiness?

**Think about how you can kickstart
your day with kindness.**

Reflect on ways to include a random act of kindness into your morning routine, whether it's leaving a positive note for a family member or helping with a chore without being asked.

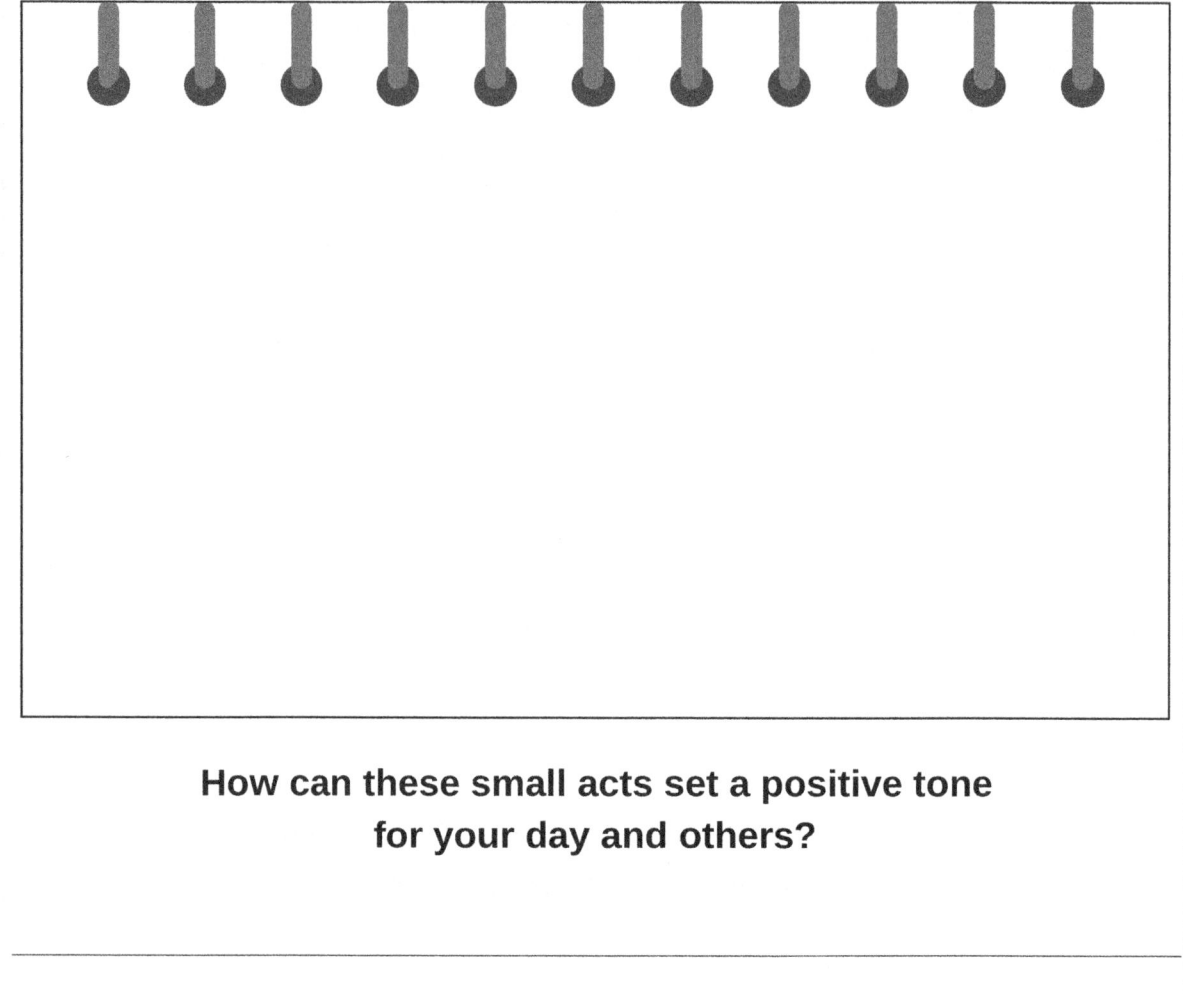

**How can these small acts set a positive tone
for your day and others?**

_____

_____

_____

_____

Consider how you can end your day on a kind note.
Reflect on ways to include a random act of kindness into your bedtime routine, such as expressing gratitude or offering a comforting gesture to a sibling or parent.

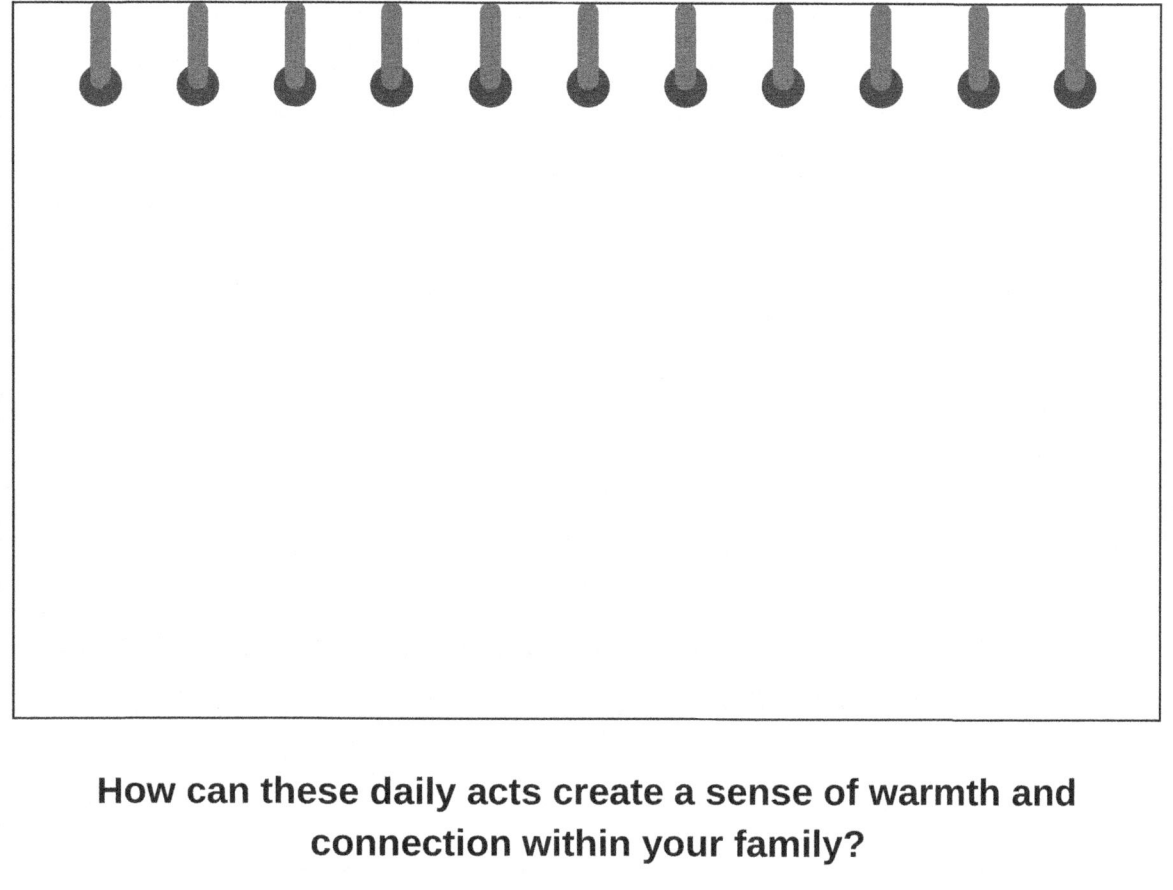

How can these daily acts create a sense of warmth and connection within your family?

___
___
___
___
___
___

Imagine doing one kind thing every day, like sending a friendly note or helping a friend with homework.
Reflect on how these daily acts of kindness can create a ripple effect.

_____
_____
_____
_____
_____

How might your positive actions inspire others to do kind things too, making the world around you a brighter and happier place?

_____
_____
_____
_____
_____
_____
_____

**Consider compliments as reflections of
the good you see in others.**
Reflect on how your compliments act like a "kindness mirror," showing people their unique and special qualities.

How might your uplifting words boost someone's confidence and bring a little extra sunshine into their day?

_____
_____
_____
_____
_____
_____
_____
_____

Think about a time when someone's kindness made you feel special.

Share how kindness has the power to create magic in our lives.

How might small acts of kindness, like a smile or a helping hand, brighten someone's day and make a big difference?

_____

_____

_____

_____

_____

_____

Reflect on a time when someone was unkind to you.
How could you respond with kindness instead of negativity?

Consider the power of transforming unkindness into kindness. How might your actions influence the other person's behavior?

Imagine kindness as a shield that protects you from unkind words or actions.
Reflect on how you can respond to unkindness by using your kindness shield.

_____
_____
_____
_____
_____
_____
_____

How might your positive and understanding attitude help others?

_____
_____
_____
_____
_____
_____

**Imagine giving compliments as colorful confetti that brightens someone's day.
Reflect on how sharing kind words can create a joyful "compliment carnival" around you.**

_____

_____

_____

_____

How could your positive comments make others feel appreciated and valued?

Imagine you had a million dollars as a dream fund for spreading kindness.

Share your wildest dreams of generosity, such as funding community playgrounds, surprising neighbors, or creating a kindness chain reaction.

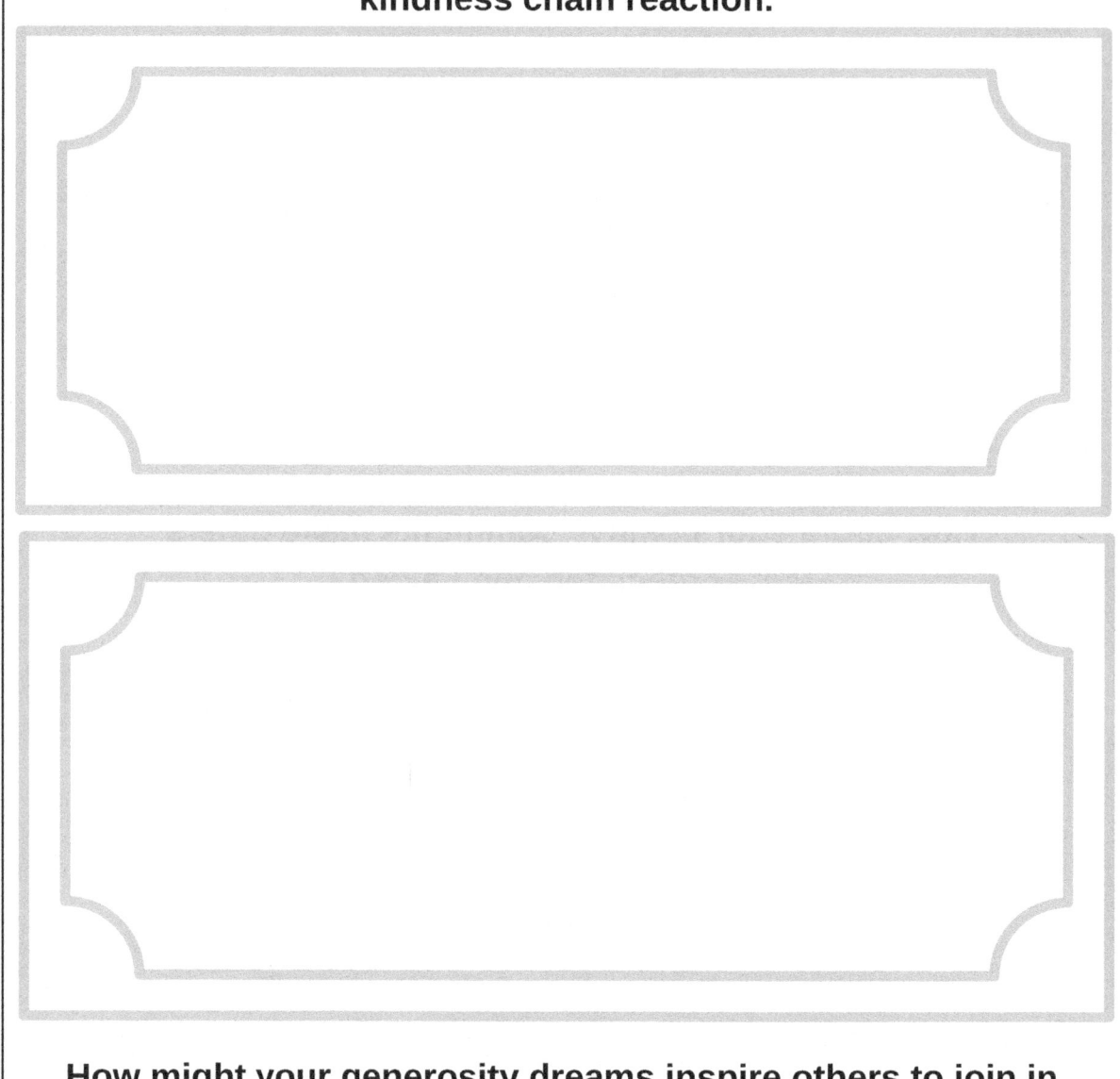

How might your generosity dreams inspire others to join in, creating a world filled with compassion and goodwill?

_____

_____

Imagine kindness as a gentle butterfly fluttering through someone's life.
Reflect on how a single act of kindness can create ripples, much like the butterfly effect.

_____

_____

_____

_____

_____

How might your kindness change someone's life, setting off a chain reaction of positivity and warmth?

_____

_____

_____

_____

_____

_____

Consider the impact a kind word can have on someone's life.

Reflect on how your encouraging words can uplift, inspire, and make a lasting difference.

How could your kindness serve as a guiding light, bringing positivity and brightness to someone's journey?

THE RIPPLE EFFECT
A KINDNESS JOURNAL
TO SPARK JOY AND COMPASSION

KINDNESS QUOTES

Kindness quotes provide us with insight and inspiration from our favorite celebrities and heroes.

- Read the quote at the top of each page.
- Take a moment to reflect on what the author meant when they made the statement.
- Try to find a connection to your own life or an emotion you can relate to.

Each page contains two questions to further your reflection.

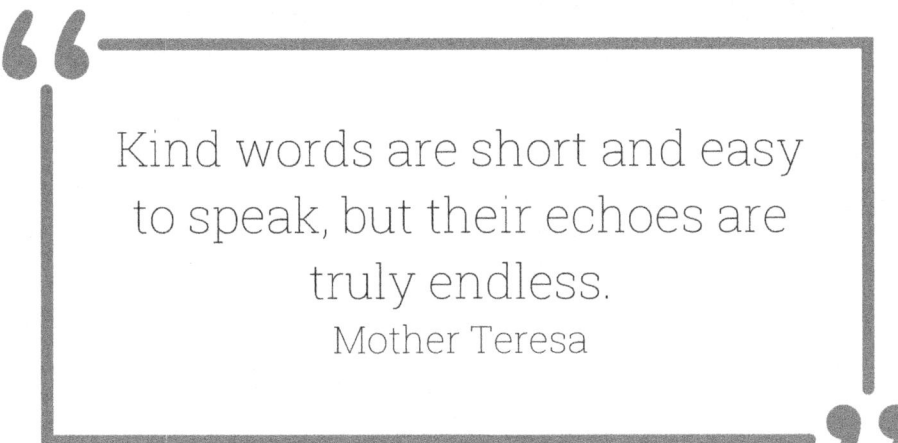

> Kind words are short and easy to speak, but their echoes are truly endless.
> Mother Teresa

> No act of kindness,
> no matter how small,
> is ever wasted.
> Aesop

What do you consider to be small acts of kindness?

_____

_____

_____

_____

_____

Why are "small" acts of kindness as important as "big" ones?

_____

_____

_____

_____

_____

_____

_____

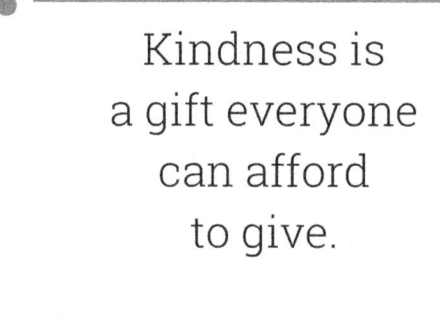

How can kindness be considered a gift?

What kindness can you share without spending any money?

What does "Sprinkle Kindness like confetti" make you think of?

_____
_____
_____
_____
_____

How can you sprinkle kindness?

_____
_____
_____
_____
_____
_____
_____
_____

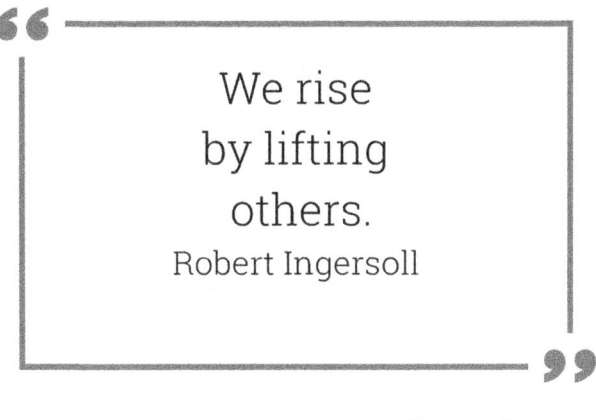

> We rise by lifting others.
> Robert Ingersoll

What are some ways you can help others?

How does helping each other make the world a better place?

> In a world where you can be anything, be kind.

Why is it so important to be kind?

_____
_____
_____
_____

What does this quote mean to you?

_____
_____
_____
_____
_____
_____
_____

> "Sometimes miracles are just good people with kind hearts."

What does a "kind heart" look like?

**Do you feel you have a kind heart?
Reflect on your reasons for feeling this way.**

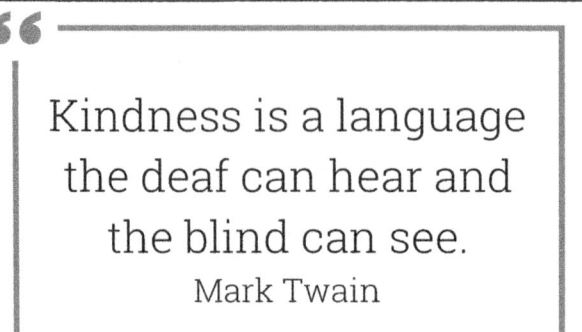

What do you think Mark Twain meant by this?

What does this quote mean to you?

> One kind word can change someone's entire day.

Create a list of things you can say that will change someone's day in a positive way.

Share a moment when someone said something nice and it changed your day.

> Sometimes the smallest things take up the most room in your heart.
> Winnie the Pooh

How does this quote remind you of kindness?

_____
_____
_____
_____

What acts of kindness have meant the most to you?

_____
_____
_____
_____
_____
_____
_____
_____

> Be kind,
> even on
> your bad days.

Why is being kind harder on bad days?

How does being kind help make your bad days better?

> "Carry out a random act of kindness, with no expectation of reward, safe in the knowledge that one day someone might do the same for you.
> Princess Diana

How does this quote change the way you think about helping others?

How have you been shown kindness?

> A single act of kindness throws out roots in all directions, and the roots spring up and make new trees.
> Amelia Earhart

How can one act of kindness inspire more kindness?

What do you think of when you read this quote?

> Sometimes all we need is a little kindness.

Write about a time when you needed kindness.

_____
_____
_____
_____

Were you shown kindness? How did it make you feel?

_____
_____
_____
_____
_____
_____
_____

> "By helping others, we help ourselves."

How has showing kindness helped you?

What does this quote mean to you?

> Kindness is not an act, it's a lifestyle.

How can making kindness a part of every day change your life?

_____
_____
_____
_____

What do you think the author meant by this statement?

_____
_____
_____
_____
_____
_____

> Sometimes it only takes one act of kindness and caring to change a person's life.
> Jackie Chan

What acts of kindness could mean this much?

_____
_____
_____
_____
_____
_____

How does this change the importance of kindness?

_____
_____
_____
_____
_____
_____
_____

> "Kindness means building bridges instead of walls."

What does this quote mean to you?

How can kindness "build bridges"?

> "A kind friend is the right kind of friend."

Why should kindness be an important part of friendships?

Who is your kindest friend? What makes them kind?

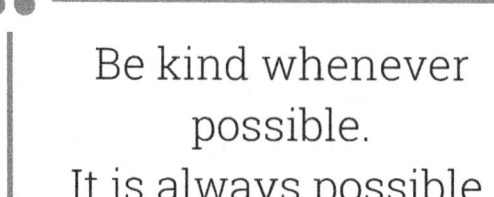

> Be kind whenever possible.
> It is always possible.
> Dalai Lama

Is there a time when you could have been more kind?

_____
_____
_____
_____

Share a time when you wish someone had been more kind to you.

_____
_____
_____
_____
_____
_____
_____

THE RIPPLE EFFECT
A KINDNESS JOURNAL
TO SPARK JOY AND COMPASSION

ACTS OF KINDNESS

Random Acts of Kindness aren't always planned out. However, you can improve your kindness habit with planning and reflection.

When you take the time to think about the person who will be receiving your kindness, each experience becomes more meaningful. The next section will help you identify acts of kindness you can share with the people in your life.

- Reflect on the type of list and examples at the top of each page.
- Take a moment to consider the people in your life and what types of kind acts you could plan to share with them.
- Challenge yourself to complete each list.

Consider your skills.
What are the best ways you can help others?

Kindness for Friends

Add to the list below

- *Give someone a compliment.*
- *Spend time with your friends and laugh together.*
- *Share a snack with a friend.*
- *Have a spontaneous 30 second dance party with your friends.*

Kindness for Family
Add to the list below

- *Write a letter saying thank you to a family member.*
- *Help prepare a meal.*
- *Play a game with a family member.*
- *Pick flowers to put in your house.*
- *Read a story to someone.*

Kindness for Animals

Add to the list below

- *Create a bird feeder out of cereal.*
- *Offer to pet sit for a neighbor.*
- *Donate blankets to a local animal shelter.*
- *Bake dog biscuits and give to the dogs in your life*
- *Pick up litter in your neighborhood.*

Kindness for The Environment
Add to the list below

- Pick up litter in your neighborhood.
- Create a poster to share the importance of taking care of the world.
- Use a recyclable bag for shopping.
- Do yard work for a family member or neighbor.
- Visit a Farmer's Market.

Kindness for Yourself
Add to the list below

- *Give yourself a compliment.*
- *Find a hobby you love.*
- *Draw a picture.*
- *Spend time with a friend.*
- *Make a list of things you are proud of.*

THE RIPPLE EFFECT
A KINDNESS JOURNAL
TO SPARK JOY AND COMPASSION

PRACTICE KINDNESS

The best way to develop a kindness habit is to practice.
Kindness is a skill.

The more you practice, the easier it becomes. One strategy to improve your kindness habit is to reflect on the kindness you have shown to others. This will help you better understand the effect kindness has on everyone.

The questions in the next section will help you learn more about the impact kindness can have.

To complete the next section, choose an act of kindness you can share with someone. Make a plan, then share the kindness. Once the kindness has been shared, answer the questions on the page to reflect on the experience.

> Write a thank you letter to someone who is important to you.

Why did you choose to thank this individual? What have they done to help you?

> Create a poster with your favorite kindness quote and hang it where others can see it.

What quote did you choose?
Why do you think others will like it, too?

> Try not to
> complain at
> all today.

**Was it hard to avoid complaining?
Did you notice a difference in your attitude?**

_____

_____

_____

_____

_____

_____

_____

_____

_____

> Leave positive notes for someone to find.

Do you think it would be inspiring to find a note?

> Make a gift for someone you care about.

How does it feel to give someone a gift you made?

___
___
___
___
___
___
___
___
___
___
___
___
___

> Make a snack to share with your friends.

How does it make you feel to share with others?

> Make a list of things you are grateful for.

How does being grateful make you feel?

_____
_____
_____
_____
_____
_____
_____
_____
_____

> Offer to help a family member.

What was their response when you offered to help?

> Pick up
> litter or trash
> at your school or
> in your neighborhood.

**How did the area look when you were done?
Why do you think this is important**

> Cheer on someone who is struggling.

How does it make you feel to see someone become successful?

> Tell someone
> a joke or
> a silly story.

How does it feel to make someone laugh?

> Teach someone a new skill.

How did you feel while helping someone learn?

> Ask someone
> to tell you stories
> about their life.

**What kind of stories did they tell?
What did you learn?**

> Create a
> piece of art to
> share with a friend.

How did it feel to create something artistic for someone you care about?

> Smile
> as much as you can
> today.

How does it feel when someone smiles back at you?

_____
_____
_____
_____
_____
_____
_____
_____
_____
_____
_____

> Give a
> big hug to
> someone you
> care about.

How does hugging someone change the way you feel?

_____
_____
_____
_____
_____
_____
_____
_____
_____
_____
_____

> Sort your
> toys and books
> to find some
> to donate.

**How does it feel to know your items
will bring joy to others?**

_____

_____

_____

_____

_____

_____

_____

_____

> Pay someone a compliment.

How did giving a compliment make you feel?

> Create a kindness challenge for your family. Encourage them to show kindness, too!

How does it feel to see people you love showing kindness to each other?

_____
_____
_____
_____
_____
_____
_____
_____
_____

> Write someone a note, just to say hello.

How does writing a note to someone you care about make you feel?

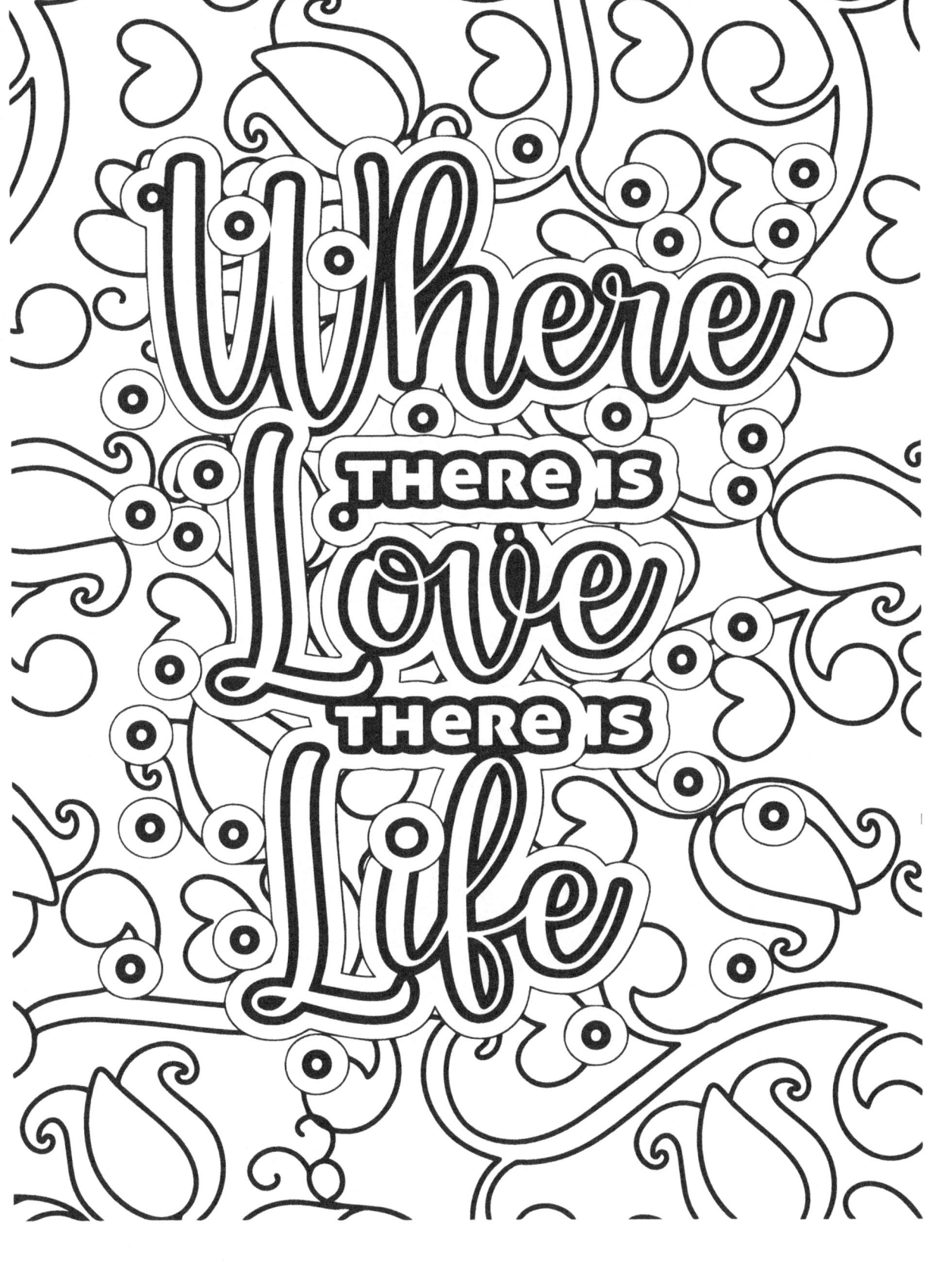

BEHIND MIGHTY MINDSETS

Mission Statement

MightyMindsets is dedicated to helping individuals, families, & communities develop healthy mindsets to grow and thrive.

When we focus on developing healthy mindsets, we build the skills to become strong community members. *Our world needs more of this right now.* The Mighty Mindset products are designed to support individuals as they embrace growth mindset, kindness, gratitude, mindfulness, and self care.

Thoughtfully bringing resilience, strength, and confidence to the people we love.

The Mighty Mindsets team is dedicated to helping others develop healthy mindsets and positive attitudes, stretching their current boundaries and comfort zones to reach success. To meet this need, the Mighty Mindsets team has created activities, journals, and mini curriculum to share strategies for this personal growth.

The team has put countless hours of research and practice into finding strategies that will build essential character traits. Products are developed with research from evidence based practices. These products support individuals as they learn, practice, and develop skills to face challenges and struggles.

"It is absolutely possible for one person to make a difference in the world. By believing in your dream and sharing it with others, even the smallest ripples you make will be felt by those across the sea."
Bethany C. Goding

Never let anything stop you from trying the impossible.

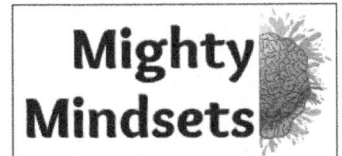

www.MightyMindsets.com

Made in United States
Orlando, FL
05 August 2024